salmonpoetry

Diverse Voices from Ireland and the World

My Kindred
Paulann Petersen

Published in 2023 by
Salmon Poetry
Cliffs of Moher, County Clare, Ireland
Website: www.salmonpoetry.com
Email: info@salmonpoetry.com

ISBN 978-1-915022-35-6

Cover Image: *Fourré, by Robert Gamblin*
Cover Design & Typesetting: *Siobhán Hutson Jeanotte*

Printed in Ireland by Sprint Print

For Ken,

my advocate

For my dear sister-poet Andrea Hollander,

and for my dear brother-poet Lex Runciman:

their wise counsel helped shape this book.

Contents

Inhabited

A big-leaf maple imprints
the pronged shape, the vein-tracery
of its deciduous leaf-children
into my eyes.

Two barred owls call
back and forth, posing a question
off to my left, its answer
far to my right.

A sister who echos my aging bones,
the wind-swaled fir
first moans, then creaks.

What to do, but invite them all
to come and live
                    here, inside me?

I taste tannin, smell resin
in each out-let breath. My inner ear
rings with the tongue of raptors.

First Task

To sweep from my front porch
fallen blossoms. What falls
from the hanging basket of fuchsias.
What drops from the planters
lining the porch's north edge.

With a wooden-handled,
corner-scraping straw broom,
to eliminate what a plant no longer needs.

To sweep away illusion.
A flower is not too lovely to fail.
No matter how much I strive, I cannot
make this entryway's garden ever-lush.
Fallen petals are crushed to wet pulp
under the broom's scour.

To sweep away my attachment
for the blown and moist and fragrant sex
of a flower. With even, long strokes,
to take the occasional shed leaf.
Bits of grime.

To create an openness
ready for a next spent bloom
to fall. An emptiness
where I can place my feet.
To waylay my urge
      until tomorrow's morning is here.
         I must wait
to sweep again.

My Muse

—A wolf does not appear to us
unless it wants to tell us something.

—a Heiltsuk belief

On the Alaska Fur Shop label
inside each jacket, stole, and cape
my grandfather made,
a she-wolf lived.
With every garment of animal skins,
she made herself seen—
her silhouette outlined by tiny gray stitches.
Throughout my childhood, she threw her head back,
opened her jaws, and keened to me
without ever making a sound.

When I finally began to write poems,
she told me, in no uncertain words.
To what I make, she is sister.
She and my poems speak the same tongue.
Both have guard-fur glinted by silver,
thick coats mantled with pollen.
Both slip through the night
to bare their throats, to sing.

Late Summer, Last Light

Silence. The trees, not strictly immobile,
but almost so. Movement so slight
only they themselves
have a feel for it.

A farthest thing from everlasting light
cuts into them, takes a sidelong path
through cedar, fir, maple.

Just now having heard my mind
sound out those five letters of its name,
the maple nods an oversized leaf at me,
signaling enough is enough
with this stillness.
This seeming nonexistence.

*

The maple knows I have come
here at the edge of trees
to practice my green death.
Which has nothing to do
with dying. Which has everything
to do with how little I know
about my own impending
non-life—this practice of stillness
my trial run at tree-breathing.

Right now, as I tell this, I rehearse
a maple-breath let out
and out and out without ever
pulling it back in.

*

The cedar can stand still the way
a corpse lies unmoving.
But cedar-stillness is not
a lack of life,
is not even a sleep, a doze,
a sleight-of-eye nap.

The cedar's stillness
isn't. I practice
its motionless soundless
breathing. What I would—
any other day—exhale,
I breathe in. Then breathe out
what my lungs profess
to crave.

*

I mimic the hundred-foot queen fir,
her inch-by-inch living—
that imperceptible candling
at her bough-tips,
her cones ripening
at their ancient amber rate.
Existence so slow
my loved ones believe
I'm not alive at all.

How little my family knows
of the mouth in each
resin-pore of my body—
countless small sister-tongues
licking the air.

To My Coffin-Tree

You will have taken a century or so to grow
a cavity in your trunk large enough to house
a dead woman this tall and broad.
You will have given yourself
over to cleave and groan, sundered
yourself open, the rift in you gaining
moreso and moreso until it can
swallow me.

I'm near ready to rest
inside you, willing to let
ensuing seasons close over me
with scales of cambium and bark.

Take me in
as part of your heartwood.

Be my own
numen of in-doing.
Do me in.

If My People Had Totems,
My Pole Would Include

A wolf.
To be the sibling I never had,
a rough-furred sister keening songs into my ear.

A hummingbird.
Because—inside a tiny cotton-lined box—
I keep the still perfect yet perfectly still body
of a hummer who long ago flew
into a windowpane. Tiny dollop of gleam,
almost weightless drop of stopped iridescence,
she lies within her cardboard casket
that once held a piece of jewelry—
this little bijou laid out on white.

A swan.
To remind me, ever the ugly duckling,
of what I did not, will never, become.

A sea-cow.
Because one took me in, eye to eye,
through an aquarium's thick glass. Me in murky air,
her under water. For whole minutes, she—
of the gorgeous name *Manatee*—gave haven
to my gaze while she nibbled her lunch.
With broad whiskered lips, she pulled apart and ate
a whole, loosely bound head of lettuce.
Leaf by swaying green leaf.

A magpie.
To show me a second way to sing.
Her trickster beak wide open,
she swallows the sun whole.

Grave Goods

Buried with upper arms
circled in gleaming bracelets,
with serpentine chains hung from their necks,

sent down with their own weapons—
finely honed and etched bronze,

accompanied by a turquoise-trimmed
comb and mirror, a silver ear-pick,
an ivory-handled knife to pare long nails,
a 24 karat penis-shield,

interred with as many coins—
each a small glowing sun—
as needed to reach the far shore:

even in death
the rich manage to own
what's most precious.

Who but the poor would collect
the powder dropped from a dangle of anthers?
Who but the un-moneyed would plunder
a forest's marginal swales,
glean a meadow plush with bloom,
shake that fine dust into a deerskin pouch,
then stow it away?
                    Fall, winter,
summer, spring, no matter.
The beloved's body goes into the earth
          flecked with pollen,
that weightless gold.

If I Were Money

I'd be descended from something
once precious enough to offer a god.

Turquoise, perhaps.
Cowries or stone beads.
Pelts of sable, ermine, marten.
Saffron, cinnamon, cloves, in packets.
Pekoe, oolong, or darjeeling tea.
All worthy enough ancestors.
But no, I'd want to be

the kin of that once-precious staple
now dismissed as commonplace,
forgettably plain. Me, descended
from an ancient currency
needing to be covered
to keep it from melting away.

I'd be an extract
from a warm-blooded sea—
a small block of salt
wrapped in soft
animal skin.

Kinship

A few of our world's people still speak
a tongue so old its closest analog
is birdsong. And a bird carved
some thirty thousand years ago
may well be our first work of art.

Why mimic the palaver of a thrush?
From wood or stone, why shape
a tern's body, its wings pressed
tight against its sides? Or remember
the dream-moments our beating arms
took hold in air, lifting us away
from earth trod smooth by our feet?

We each possess a bird-soul.
On the highest branch of every family tree,
a winged spirit preens in the sun,
gleaming with iridescence—
that sheen of our common blood.

A Backstory Beyond My Recounting

Unaccountably old, the world is a world class
self-starter, ever used to making itself anew
again and again out of the makings of itself—
from that first stellar stuff.

I must take care in such a world—
careful of where I place my feet,
of what I pick up, of how I use
the pen gleaming so old in my hand.

I'm writing myself onto this paper
that was once a pine that was cone
that was cloud not so long before having been
ocean that was the prior glint of rain.
With care I must choose the words
to write onto this sea
that too is a seed that too
is the sky's overcast.

This moment's ink lays down its darkness,
giving off a wet light before it dries.
The pen in my hand has—just five words ago—
contrived to make that mark of its own name,
and now will do so one more time
before I end, calling itself
Reconfigured Star.

Household

—for Gaston Bachelard's *The Poetics of Space*

i.

Headed inside, I become twins. With a touch
from the right hand, one of me opens the door.
To the small god of thresholds, I make my offering—
two pods of star anise, a forked branch of basil—
intoning, *Breathe in, little god, breathe in.*
I weigh the apotheosis of doorknobs and keys.

With the left hand's fingertips, my other self
closes the door behind me—entry making me
both open *and* closed.

ii.

Double, I am now inside the house that is me.
One lamp burns day and night. The star of me.
My mouthful of light. A swallow of blood-honey
I hold within the black of my body.

My upper story rises above my lower.
Stairs are narrow, steep. I step each riser,
up or down, listen for the creak.
This sound announces the split in darkness
as it opens to surround my climb, my plunge.

iii.

Mine is the house of winter, the oldest of seasons.
Only age makes the time to hear those tales
that cannot be told spring, summer, or fall.
End-day stories. Only winter holds the embryo leaf
inside the node within a naked branch's tip.

A pocket's lint-cornered warmth, this house
lets me stay alive in the world despite
the world's intentions on my life.

iv.

This space makes itself from pairs of mirrors,
each staring into the other's quicksilver eyes.
Haven made of timbers in which yellow blood
still rises. Created from its very own
tatters and scrapings,
its dust and unguent and musk.

Two magpies—not white, not black, but both—
emerge from under the dome of their hive-hold nest
to fly outside through one of the half-open windows.
Even as these windows frame each mote, mottle,
and mettlesome of the Elsewhere, they contain
a world's vastness.

v.

A bird and a bird: feathered black, feathered white,
oiled with time's iridescence:
I am both.

Death and one more day for living: these I am,
in the same. Flying away, flown in, I stir air
into the breath making these words.

My *Being*
being both here
and gone.

My Page in the Book of Concurrences

Half sunken, half reaching into air,
maybe I'm the ribs
of a great ship left stranded
long ago in shoreline, keel now far under—
a big-bodied cradle at sea's edge,
sand-steady, just a little sigh and sigh,
wind-harp rocking.
             Maybe I'm lighter than sighs,
ready to float at less than a moment's notice,
a flower-petal of feather
morning glory white, kite bright.
                     Or mist

buckling itself up the headlands,
rolling into tree-caught clouds,
or sand working out
a level-headedness,
shape-shifting each imprint.
             Perhaps I'm water
coming in and in, high tide,
then out and low, but always *somewhat* in,
somewhat out, swell and dash,
salty singing.
         Both everywhere at once
and fallen on each spot, exactly,
maybe I'm sweet and bound toward
the aggregate of my choosing.
             Maybe, I'm rain.

ii

Unfurling

my soul among all souls
lives in a silver vein
coursing the chthonic world

lives in that ore containing both living and dead
amid their mercurial being

my soul runs its thread of silver
with the huge cedar-neighbor's shining thread
alongside that of the great-horned owl
the wing-flash flicker

mine, a wisp of gleam
within the precious metal-light
of Rilke, of Gandhi, of Sappho
of my Whitman father, my Whitman mother

what surrounds our vein of souls
is solid, is the sky
the mountain tarn
a lily-meadow endless in its petal-thick perfume

one vein, one pathway we all take
through the underside of a world
          unfolding even now
       unfurling ever

this world that uncoiled its worldliness
long before I was,
           before *birth* itself
             could be born

The World After

—Surely our parents give birth to us twice,
the second time when they die.

—Anaïs Nin

My second birth comes parceled out
in two halves. First, my father.
His death reaches me
on an early March morning.
A phone call. His suffering finished,
done. What to do
but partly start over
with only half the parents
I've had my whole life?
Try to begin anew
with the still-living one.

Seven years go by.
I sit beside my mother's self
made wooden by Alzheimer's.
I hear her last breath—
ragged intake, soughed release.
In November cold, the second half
of my second birth is done.
Me, fully-delivered once more.

In this afterward world
I stand alone. Too new, too raw
even to fill my lungs
and let loose
a first cry.

Omen

—*for my mother, Grace Whitman*

On what will turn out to be your
early winter death-day,
I look out a window and see
what had early in May freighted itself
with purple incardescence, drenched itself
in high-priestess perfume. A *lilac*—
at one branch's tip—
                            now impossibly
                                    in blossom.

Vastly early or late,
it bursts into my eyes:
an apparition beyond my ken.

No telling how I can tell,
but I know this day will unfurl
another blooming—
a terrible beauty so untimely
I will not outlive
its passing.

My Parents' Ashes

Mostly they're dust.
One fine enough to color
whatever it touches. A powder
that muffles every gleam—
one intent on taking to the air
and flying away into nothing.

But also bits of bone.
Chips. Nubs. Tiny beads.

This slight scree must be *sacrum*,
that bone least likely to burn, leaving
its small shards after the pyre
smolders shut.

Words on this page, carry
my father and mother, my Whitmans.
Be the seeds that remain
when burning is done.
Be sacrums, too. Make
this much of my parents
stay alive.

The Glass-Bender

—for my father, Paul Whitman

Nighttime in this city of my birth,
and I search for what little neon remains,
signs that you could have made in the early 50's
after you'd learned to bend neon, teaching yourself
to turn a single length of glass tubing
into even-lettered, artful words, before blacking out
all but the parts that needed to glow
to make the message clear.

Pulsing from a few store windows,
the red of OPEN   OPEN   OPEN
is the only neon left for me to see.
These signs proclaim *Already Unlocked,*
yet command me to *Unlock What's Closed.*

Hand-shaped, your numen bends
its light toward my eyes.

Because

these eyes seeing my father's young image
are now as old as his eyes
ever became:

one more way I outlive my parents:

if I look closely enough
at this photo of him taken before I was
even born, his eyes flame
with what he already counted on:

outliving him
was all he ever wanted from me:

to be, for my entire life, at least one
easeful step this side of poverty, as he was not:

to wear a mortar board and gown,
to pause on stage long enough
for a dean to place into my hands that degree
the Great Depression denied him:

to write his unwritten poems:

what he wanted because there *was* a me:

that I at some point might see the word *cause* lies
in the core of *because*:

and because of his not-in-the-least-
accidental cause,
I am here:

his life at the heart of this fire
I name *alive*

Wake

—on the sea off Mumbai

A little roil, some turmoil, enough brine
for a bit of foam, the launch's motor purling.
My fingers dig into my purse, finding
the tiny container carried with me always.
I pry it open, pinch from its contents some ash,
the hard bits too large to be called grit,
so big in their smallness I can call them
by nothing but their true name—
bones of my mother, bones of my father.
I sift them onto this flux
made by a boat
parting the water.

The Arabian Sea takes—
without hesitation—
my father, my mother.
First onto its surface in a pale streak
of cloud-glaze. Then deep into its vast self.

How quick such transformation—
bodies first eaten by fire,
then swallowed into water's body.
These cold remains of flame
become mineral food.

With who created me, I feed
a sea's dark salt blood.

Dear Walt Whitman

For you, I place a winged carving
afloat in the air. A mermaid,
she turns, idles, swings slow.
Her carved feathers, carved scales,
all plume with gold. Her breasts
are pale, bare. She holds a blue comb
in her right hand. In the other, a mirror
whose frame is painted blood red.

Below her, I set a surf of potted orchids.
The purple ones you love, the tawny rose,
those that are caps of white.

At the skylight's edge, I hang
a crescent moon. For you.

I bring a row of upright porcelain arms to the sill
of my living room window—they being
nine of the moon's own limbs.
Bare or gloved or jeweled: three times three
pale moonstone hands wave inward,
call out to the street. All for you.

Whatever lazes in pagan beauty
as well drifts in you.

Whatever blooms without calculation
unfurls in you as well.

Whatever many-handed moon
waves its multitudes
beckons—ever—in you.

You, Coreopsis

Whitman's boast, his avowed flower of furtherance,
you are short-lived, the cultivators say. But no cultivar.
Cheapest, nearest, easiest, like the poet himself
you go and grow wild where you can. Most call you
tickweed, your seeds crazy to beggar themselves
when they can hitch a ride on fur or feather or cuff.

Whitman takes bumptious pains to tell me
you bloomed ahead of him, blazing his pathway
wherever his travels took him west.
But can I take him, the New World Braggart,
at his word? Yes.

An oriole heartbeat thrummed in C Sharp,
a hillock's sunburned thigh, you are lime and molasses
bottom-heavy in my breath, a nip of anise and yellow musk.

Brazen, unfurled, you beckon to me—unspooling
your blooms, making for me a far and fire-bright road.
A way to resist you? No.
Cheap and nearly too easy, I follow.

Whitman. Me. Hermes.

—with homage to Rilke's "Orpheus. Eurydice. Hermes."

His hand clasping mine, the ankle-wing god leads me up,
away from subterranean sorrow, shows me the way
to follow you, the Good Gray Poet—
your song enough to return me soon to light.
My open eyes fix on the darkness ahead,
as if I could watch your back
leaning into the climb.

You already know. Unlike the god,
you must take no notice of me, must keep
your vision pointed forward, eyes fast
on what your burgeoning sight can embrace.
You are, though, given leave to hear me.
My whispered footfalls. The wisps of half-song
I begin to make in your wake.
You, who fetch me up
from songless dark.

Since birth, I've borne your name,
as if your mother or sister, wife or daughter.
Am I your Eurydice too? Unlike her,
my sex will not fold its asphodel petals
in on itself, will not close. You lead me
into another virginity, an old woman's aching womb
waiting to be broken, filled and broken open again.
Pregnant with unborn songs.

My white hair drifts into my eyes. I brush it away,
trying to see your gray hair spilling over your nape,
down the back of your linsey coat.

The messenger-god's grip on my hand tightens.
We must be near the opening into daylight.
Already I can smell air weighted by rain.

Keen, you listen for the thrust of my leaves
toward the sun, leaves poised to sprout,
to sidle their green,
                        leaves eager to sing.
You do not look back.

Why, in My Grave, What Once Was Me
Will Hold a Wolf Amulet

Because the she-wolf's coat is coarse.
Because her fur is festooned with long guard-hairs,
stiff and silvered. Because she takes in the sun,
her coat gleaming with day's light.

She catches this shine and funnels its heat
down into her skin. She feasts
on the warm-blooded world.

Because she—a changeling of colors—
slides through the night with a moon riding
full on her back. Because that moon
knows her as its familiar,
its light and the sun's light
being half-sisters.

Because—to tell me what's what—
she seeks me out more often than I deserve.

Because—even though her teats are swollen,
her whelps nearby—she sometimes will tarry
long enough to be my muse.

Moan-growling, she nips, draws a bead of red
from my outstretched hand. Then licks it away,
reminding me, yet again:

Words are my talismans—scent-tracking
their way toward me. Each is a glinted eye
piercing the dark. Each throws its head back,
yowling its open-throated song.
Every word is a den of ink
dug into a pale page.

iii

Moon

I'm the sky's one orchid

the dark animal's silver claw

an ear cupped
    for the hearsay of another's light

pewter pawprint above the horizon

the night's steadfast changeling

song of a single bell
    the moment before it's rung

Lake

Unlidded eye of the underworld,
I stare ever upward, taking the sky on.
Taking on clouds, their chameleon twists.
Donning the sun, spreading its flares.
Wearing the hawk in flight.

On my surface lives the moon
in one iteration or another,
the spilled milk of stars. On me reside
the fringe of trees at my edge,
rocks, grasses, the deer come to drink,
the raccoon washing her long-fingered hands.

I am an eye feeding that brain
deep in the earth's huge skull.
Brain of underground wellings, of tuneless
chthonic songs. A lava fumarole brain,
its molten stem sparks with what—
on my quavered sheen—I can see.

Moths Have Their Say

For millions of years, our mother, the Moon,
was enough for our whole family. We found our way
by first finding her place in the vast night air.
We hid by day, asleep on leafy undersides.

Of fur-bearing clans, we were oldest and most small.
Painted with huge eyes, our wings sometimes carried color,
mostly not. Our antennas mimed the fronds of tiny ferns.

Whose upstart idea was it to break away, to doze at night?
To navigate by that hot-lamp in the sky?
To take on every lurid color under its rays?
Butterflies, that's who, a branch of our family
grown far astray.

Cinnabar, Antler, Emperor Gum,
White Witch, Atlas, Great Owlet,
Death's Head: we moths came first.

Except for the light our Moon borrows
each night, we can take or leave
that show-off, the Sun.

This Is the Snake

who latches onto her own tail to hold
the world's end and beginning together,

who sings Rimrock,
Juniper, Jackrabbit, Sage into being,

who is double-headed
so she can swim the lake
with two eyes fixed on the sun,

whose handprint is only a thumb,

whose skin is obsidian mirror,

who bleeds a monthly
rainbow of blood,

whose halo gives the moon its shadow.

Deep in her body, womb and grave
share a single space.

She Who Makes Her Nest
from Frankincense and Myrrh

Her remains sift, her ashes
merging with the nest's conflagrated char,
that sticky relic left when flame takes its leave
from the resin of trees growing
in ancient cases.

With air-hungry wings,
the Phoenix rises, bearing aloft
what's left from those precious oils—
the perfume drawn from a sum
of her countless deaths.

Her Sister Tells Water What's What

You're so full of yourself
when you're rain—a little bit of you
everywhere all at once.

I know. I know.
To be all places at the same time
and *not* be conceited?
That would be more than hard.
But you won't even try.

When you're a lake, you gather
every scrap of moonlight for yourself,
sending it gleaming across your flat belly.
A river, you play catch-me-if-you-can,
working to wear down
a canyon's roots.

About being ocean, you go on and on.
You've always just got back from,
or are on your way to, being a sea.
All that essential motion.
Lapping and rocking and lapping
as if you were the one and only female
with salt tucked into a not-so-secret spot,
the only woman waiting
for the world's tongue
to find her out.

How the Sun Gets Those Flares

Before you can hear any of this,
you must first understand:
the sun is *female*. Sun-Woman
is her name. And that does *not* make—
by default—the moon a man. No.
In fact, the sun and moon
are half-sisters. Easy to see that.

True enough, many stars are male.
Most, in fact. But they're so far away from her
they don't really count. And Sun-Woman
isn't much interested in them, anyway.

Some time ago, she took a female lover,
one who waits for her on the nether-side.
Each late afternoon, the sun inches down
toward the horizon—nonchalant,
as if she's merely listing westward.
Once she touches the horizon line,
she slips under. Quiet-like.
In minutes, she's gone.

Any fool knows what happens next.
She and her lover go at each other
red-hot crazy. How could she possibly
return at dawn unchanged? Good thing
we can't watch what they're up to.
We'd stare ourselves blind.

The Mother of All Storms

Always full-term,
she's womb-swollen
with wind and sleet
and snow ready to fly
horizontal.

Pressing her right palm
onto her belly's rise,
she can feel thunder
roil under her skin.

Raying out from the hard
bubble of her navel,
wild zig-zags of stretched flesh
flash their lightning.

Her taut skin
shines with all the yet
unfallen rain.

Eve Explains The Fall

From the start, most things
were horizontal. I didn't have to reach
up for the apple. Gleaming, it hung
at eye level. Once my teeth
grazed its blushing skin,
the serpent merely *sidled* away.

A level path led Adam and me
out the garden gate. What's called
the Fall from Grace
was more a lateral move.
One not up the stairs, or down,
but across the way.
Not higher or lower. No.
To the other side of the tracks.

I pulled my worldly goods
in the bed of a little wagon.
I *rolled* my stuff from Eden
to the forwarding address.
The road was rocky, but I could see
our route stretching out for miles.
The only mention of *falling*
came from Adam.
That whole way, he nagged me
to fall in step. Behind him.

Calypso

From sea-surge
I down ambergris, sulphur,
balm of sharp brine.
I drink song cycle, tide tempo,
moon in rote rotation,
the circle surrounding Circe.

Otter wine, kelp dander,
these I swallow, deep-breathing
a sideswipe of iodine.
With notes of far-flung pollen,
my throat intones
a tincture of spume.

My every cell saline as any sea,
I give myself over—
sure of my slurrying self.
I carry the dash of ebb and neap.
The murmur of salt-blood
thrums inside my heart.

Sixty Percent Liquid, You Belong
to that Heavenly Body Closest to Earth

Queen of Watery realms, she reigns over your spittle and tears.
Your own blood's ever-surging, sighing tide.
Your menstrual flow. Your scurried semen. All hers.

She coaxes each seed to burst its husk and become
the honey on your tongue, the meat rumbling your gut.
Her creamy light feeds each infant blossom.

Musk, mead, and sweat wring themselves
from the sponge of her flesh. Nectar too. Both venom
and the toxin's antidote. In each, she's there.

A soma-cradle, hers is the death-ship ready to pull anchor
and freight your soul onto the hidden shore.
Only she can read the sea-chart mapping

your own and fathomless dark side.

The Gardener
Learns to Live Under Water

By planting seeds in sandy soil
that was once a wide lake's bottom,
ancient lake that swallowed life after life
while its wind-riven waves ate at a shoreline.

By feeling the weight of long-ago water
pressing into her back
as she leans into her garden work.

By using her index finger to jab each seed downward.
By scissoring that finger and her thumb
to coax loose loam into making
the just-created holes disappear.

Creatures—surely countless—drowned in this lake,
then sank to its bottom, coming to rest
on the very spot where her garden stands.
Their deaths make the particulate of the soil.

Each seed she plants takes a water-weight
with it, pulls a lake's ghost into the earth.

Each lies only fractions deep,
but enough to take hold in a darkness
made from drowning.

The seed drinks up the heft of a thousand griefs.
Its first leaf, looking nothing like the leaves to follow,
sings uncountable songs.

She watches as—from a water-grave—
one small hook of new green
life rises.

A Metamorphosis of Grief

Outside her kitchen door,
on the first step going down into dusk,
the Mother places her offering:
the sole part of herself that might
summon those animals named *Mercy*.

There she sets a dish, one mounded with salt,
distillation from that overtime of her crying.
White porcelain. An odd saucer whose cup
she dropped into brokenness long ago.
Thin. Bone china that light can enter
and pass through.

Weary of grief, sodden with crying,
she wants only to sleep for deadened hours
and not wake up to the raw presence of absence.
Not waken in time to learn—all over again—
the names of what she has lost.

Gathering moisture from the air,
her mourning dish of salt
would turn itself back into tears if it could,
but instead stiffens into a small block,
piece of herself she offers on pale china.

Drawn to such reconfigured grief,
compelled to what glitters
so like a fallen star, one by one
the creatures of night approach.

Each unfurls its tongue.

Ophelia Tells of the Stream
that Inhabits Her Dreams

I see into its flux. Its scant foam.
Those pebbles along its backbone.
The sway of drowning grass
where it's taken banks
into its embrace.

Snow's blood sister,
it's a distant cousin to the clouds,
the rock's cool-fingered masseuse.
A gleam unimpeded, it can glean
every image reflected along its length.

For as long as dark reveries
have flowed into me, poured out,
it's coursed in my dreams.

Murmur. Natter. Its talk
susurrates just out of reach
when I wake.

It's the sleep-stream I see
and can see into, both at the same
timeless time.

A current of story I enter,
exit, enter,
never at will.

A Piscine

She demands to be baptized again,
this time like a Believer of old.

Not full immersion,
but with drops of sweet water
pressed into her brow
by the fingers of a Revered Woman.

Then—being washed clean,
bathed in the promise of second chances—

she'll don a skin of glittering scales,
sport five gleaming fins.
Evermore she will wear her coat
of iridescent sun-flecks,

the sleek and shining
garment of herself, reclaimed.

A Wife's Belated Bow to the Sun

A book of symbols tells me
gold is your excrement.
All this time, and I've not realized
I've been wearing your dung.
But could have known by just
looking closer. That gleam,
that readiness to flicker,
could come from only what you
were willing to expel.

Source of all light,
you give your waste away
so a bride can be given
away into marriage. Even now,
your precious castings
run circles around the base
of my left hand's fourth finger.
With nothing less than this—
your star-scat—
I to him am wed.

One of Yin's Voices Speaks Up

You'd think water's female aspect
would be a pond or a lake—
deep, reflective, still, taking
the sun and moon and clouds
onto its slick-shimmered skin.
Wrong. You would be
dead wrong. Being a woman, I know
at least that much about water.

One high-summer day, I stood
behind a waterfall, in a shallow cave
scooped out of the cliff's base.
Through the cascade, I looked out and down
at the roiling pool where the water's falling
came to its end.

Din pummeled my ears. Mist weighted
my hair. The air—smelling
of skunk cabbage, willow and mullien—
tasted fecund and wet. Deafened, mute,
I gazed through that plummet joining
a world on high to the one below,
and I knew.
                The man is rock—
still, ever still, afraid to give up
his hard-won place far above the rest.
The woman sweeps right over
his prominence. In sheer free-fall,
she heads down to earth,
hellbent to reach the sea.

Had the Matriarch Been Born a Bat

She'd grow umbrella-spine fingers
long as her whole body—what she'd need to carry
those almost transparent membranes
of her huge furless wings.

She'd give birth while dangling from her toes.
A daughter, a son, would clamber out of her
like fonts bubbling from their source.
Hanging topsy-turvy, she'd nurse those babies—
her milk letting up, not down, its heavy cream rising.

She'd spread her wings across each doorway's lintel,
becoming the threshold-keeper. Staying her hairy tongue
from idle click-chat, she'd save its length
for drinks of nectar, plunges into night's deep bloom.

Ages past—before earth and sky wrenched apart
from each other, before light even made its entry,
while night still swaggered and held sway—

her ancestors would have been the only ones
who could always find their way.

The Marriage of Zephyr and Flora

Had she merely spoken his name—
even in a sweet whisper—he could have resisted.
But she opened her mouth and lilacs poured forth.
She parted her lips and daphne spilled out.

In a tendril, honeysuckle escaped
through that moist space
between her teeth. Anemones
jostled themselves out and into the light.

Of course the Gentle West Wind
gathered her wafting perfume
to keep as his own. Of course the god
stilled himself to watch a garden rush
from her flushed lips.

What burst from the deep cave
of her mouth was a verdant fire,
the ember of pistil and stamen—
such color as only burning can create.
Zephyr was *made* to fan that flame,
to breathe it into a blaze.

He could do nothing else but marry her.
He had to see—could not bear never knowing—
what brimmed from her other darkness, below.

Pursued by What Frightens Her

The story's heroine runs.
                    She throws her thick-toothed comb
behind her. It becomes a forest, a barrier dense
with straight-trunked trees.
                    Through her fingers
she lets slip
the chain of her silver necklace.
It meanders itself into becoming
a sun-gleamed river, a current
that must be forded.
                    Over her shoulder,
she flings a strand of gray hair glinting
on her jacket's dark lapel.
It weaves itself into the web
of a boulder-sized spider.
                    She runs faster,
in her wake releasing her favorite purple scarf,
the scent of perfume
she's pressed into her nape
thickening its weave. Her scarf creates
a narrow field of lavender-drowse
that must—by what's closing in on her—
be crossed.
                    Weary, she falters,
she stumbles, until she remembers
to leave behind

her shadow.

Cut loose from her body,
it lengthens and widens until its darkness
swallows her fright. *Whole.*

She can slow. Walk. Stroll.

The One Who Brings
the Sun Back to Us

Her antlers curve out and up
like a bowl-shaped crown balanced on her head.
Born far, far to the north, this reindeer doe—unlike the stag—
doesn't shed her rack come November. She keeps it
for the task she'll undertake in winter's grip.

At solstice, the sun has swung so low it teeters
at the world's edge. Only the one who nurtures new life
can be called upon to retrieve it. No bare-headed stag can recover
something so cold it's become a milky pool frozen
to the sky. Only the Deer Mother will do.

Dropping her hoar-frosted head,
the doe scoops that frigid ball of dwindled light
into her antlers' embrace. Climbing higher in the southern sky,
our sun-bearer brings us—slow step by slow step—
the gleam and warmth of lengthened days.

Signs of Where She Once Was Going

When the world was still soft, when the world
could be shaped at will,
                       the serpent went
side-sliding along—each slip-twitch
a hook in a song whose lyrics were nothing
if not one hook after another.

Where this serpent sidled and switchbacked,
where she meandered in the time of dream,
the marks left by her breath-let body
made the world—made gorge and riverbed,
bluff and arroyo, made swale and delta,
bay and island, outback and inlet.

When things were not yet hardened
into being how we know them now,
this serpent set movement into motion
at the touch of her scales.
Yes, *a She*. This serpent was that She
who gave milk, who suckled her young.

Look anywhere. Peer.
See the waves, the crenellations,
the swirl and riffle: the commotion left
from all those wormlets
who ribboned from her teats.

Reparations

Let the Sun still live
in her house named Sun-Wheel—
her no-sided, all-sided home,
a ray-roomed place of residence.

Let each of her arms reach
the curve of those rounded walls,
her fingers touching the bowed glass
of every bay window. Her home holds
so many windows that her light
can find its way out and into
the *all* of this world.

Her rays make the noise
of trumpet-vine blooms. Her beams
create both the roil of sugar ants
boiling from their hill,
and the sweetness to feed them.
She is crown and halo.
Eye of All.

Give us—who once worshipped her—
a glimmer of wisdom, the gleam
of steady restraint. Let her fierceness
be shaded by her mercy,
while we attempt
the dark work of repair.

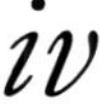

Sown

Where the earth has swallowed a star
a first corn plant grows. Each stalk
rustles with the riff of wind.
Each ear tassels, streaming its silk—
those milky wisps—into blue air.
Within, kernels bubble into constellations.
Long rows of cheek-to-cheek suns.

Where earth has swallowed
a moon, a melon plant emerges.
Tendrilled insistence. Blooms
big and yellow as an afternoon's yawn.
The fruit pale, glowing, growing
phase by phase. Mottled skin.
Sweet flesh of borrowed light.

In the spot where earth opened
to swallow a comet, a silver birch
erupts. White fire's tall column
marked with scars of blackest night,
topped by a glimmer of pale leaves.

Each season thereafter,
earth starts over. More
rooted rows of stars. New vines
strung with lunar pearls.
More trunks afire, risen.
Bursting. Green.

Some Cracks of Magic

—Be aware: there are openings that lead into the other world.

mercury   balsam
a mountain's outline against the moon

quicksilver   ash
smoke and horizon

black snake   green snake   blue snake
yellow   red   white snake
snake of no color

that rock-vein bleeding a gem
a river's exit wound
creosote's dust

travertine   bee drone
harp string   tadpole

a snake of many colors
its cloven tongue casting for scent

ozone's indigo
camphor-fissure

the vulva in an apple's heart

Lily

Drops flung from a goddess's breast
formed the Milky Way—
a strew of countless creamy stars.
A few escaped the sky's reach,
falling into our world.
Where each touched down,
it bloomed.

These white stars
learned to call our realm
their home. Fallen-to-earth milk,
they ooze perfume—sweet and thick.
An incense stolen from the sky,
that alchemist of scent.

A Tree's Mirrored Self

"As above, so below."
　　　　—an axiom from alchemy

Groping, reaching,
drinking, your roots seek—
in darkness—what's chthonic.
Hard. Dark mineral.
Watery dissolution.

As underpinning,
you prepare the way,
creating the shape
your other half will take
above ground.

Trunk, branch, twig and leaf
mirror your under-self.
Visible spirit of air,
you suckle sunlight,
sip dioxide,
tongue the ethers.

Tossing dapple-shadow
down, you are a breathing,
creak-and-sough soul
clamped to the earth
by a mirror-twin
busy delving beneath.
Creature ground-locked.
Creature soaring.

What July Drops from Her Sky

light gone strident
by lack of an overcast

light sent murmurous
by a cloud's intervention

breeze side-winding itself
under the morning's corner,
getting from today
a little rise

bird call's
pepper-tattoo

that faint tick tick tic
of a Doug fir's
spent pollen-blooms
let loose—

the sperm of giants
sudden and almost
lighter than air

Yet Leafless, the Tulip Tree Readies to Flower

The blooms have each waited
inside a small, tight bud
all winter long—each a sex-nub,

a tender, excitable mound
of tree-flesh rousing
to sunlight's rub. They've begun

to swell. Their catkin shells grow
and glow. Slow slow arousal.
Until the tree shudders into

a thousand outbursts of pink
and cream, each cupping a clot
of pollen's sticky gold.

Reckless petals fling open
wider—some already
surrendered to the ground.

Extract

Each drop brings to your tongue
sex's savor, that taste
of the all-out giving in.
Nothing but unshruggable
flower-heat.

You're eating this earth's perfume.
You've taken into your mouth
more unfurled labial petals
than you can count.

You can't count on being able
to wait a single second more.
Swallow and you set
your throat on fire.

In the Name of Decorum

This flowering plant is first
and foremost
fecund vegetation.
Its bulbous main root gives off
curling side-shoots,
pubic hair gone long and thick.
Its main stem grows
pale flagellates up its length.
Fat lateral branchlets end
in phallic cones.
Bog rhubarb, the book says,
Common butterbur.
    Such tame labels,
these names given to brazen unclothed organs—
the compendia of science demanding
we be discreet.
    In the botanist's book, no one dares
to sing the truth.
Cuntwort. Woody dick.

Urine

ancient cure for ringworm

solvent in the medieval
    deep-sided laundry tub

eau d'excess
amber dram
liqueur of sharp chartreuse

the vein of gold
    flooding your body's heat
    out of you and down into air,
    into the where of its plash

a sunflower spurting
    away from your body

your blood's cider, your flesh's brew

tincture of all
    your body is

then isn't anymore

Broadcast

A cherry tree once blown with white
now spritzes its branches with ripened
doppler-shine. And right now, there's a fine
ping on the glass-topped patio table.

Released from a somewhere
above the lattice roof layered in vine,
comes a cherry pit, picked clean. Then the fat
thonk of one with its high-gleam flesh intact.

Early summer, and robins drop
metamorph rain—bared seed, bruised fruit,
and the pink shit of Cherry-breasts gone
flat-out dowsy with feasting.

Pip. Plop. Pip.

Downfall

Like a shower of stars,
in light-streaks beyond counting,
rain plummets.

These pinpoints of gleam
disappear, join to create that oneness
called pond, lake, or bay.

Held this way, rain
makes itself into a great sleek eye
open wide to heaven.

At night, this rain-eye takes—
onto its dark pupil—the portrait of each
opal-bodied star above it.

The fallen
become an earthly mirror
for the unfallen.

Remedies

With imperceptible motion,
a lone swan's white medicinal light

glides across the sky-width of a pond.

Huge Doug firs drop
tight, redolent cones,

their pitch a healing scent stolen

from our moon's apothecary,
the sun's unlabeled vials.

A Chance

Our sun's one lidless eye
calls to those lucky eyes that follow
its arc across our sky.

The sky itself sets its fabric, the air,
into moving. Then—with any luck—
there's wind. Breeze,
if the sky's less ambitious.

And trees—if we're fortunate enough
to live where they show
enough height on a horizon
to gain the name *tree*.

And stellar jays. And cutthroat trout.
And those gnats that cloud
fallen pears.

And a blossom pink enough
to beckon long enough
that it lures into itself
a bee.

Our fortune
told in that bee.

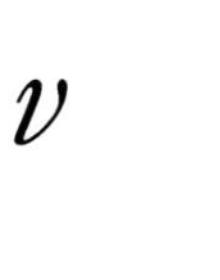

A Self-Portrait in Trope

I'm the glass twice full, more than half
    emptied, savior and supplicant, both.
Worm and dirt-warm, I'm
    sanctuary and the deserted street of grit
    leading into it, the needled firs
    I'm grateful to see
    lining that open avenue.

Heedless daughter's mother.
Hapless daughter's self.

Un-learner of habits twice as old as myself,
    pupil of habits so new
    price-tags flutter
    from each right cuff.

Conifer's confidante.
Resin's own recherché.

Bearer of a body thickened with what I have
    ever borne, I give birth
    to this newest body every morning,
    bury it in sleep each darkness,
    this thickset of myself
    waking only to dream
    and awaken again.
In that slowed motion of wakefulness,
    I let light lay its hand
    onto the steeple of fir boughs
    now alive inside
    my eyes.

In a Concurrent World

Some of the trees agree
to speak again. I listen.
Their words branch forth,
phonemes singing
first in palmate,
then in cordate.

One says she will be the Mother.
Bearer of ovate leaves, she offers
the milk of cloud-roil, of sun,
of the glistered core inside stone.
Hers will become my sole food.

She's the magnolia,
that primordial mammal.
From her leaf-heavy limbs,
stars break into bloom.

Her beneficence, her boon—
so much laden light seeping
sweetness into my throat.

Riches

May I learn to be poor
like a mole snubbing
the sun's largesse,
relying instead
on earth's deep pockets,

        or poor like the rain
with nothing to spend
but itself, not a blessed thing
to do but parcel itself out
into the smallest denominations
it can manage,

        or the scent
roused by that rain,
rising from a forest floor's
bottom line,

    or those mundane stones
given—by virtue of being
in a river's bed—
the gleam of wealth.

    Let me be the meadowlark,
       my throat
spent for song.

Piecework

Hummingbird, you pulse
and probe. Bloom by bloom
your needle-beak stitches our world
together—fine overcast stitches
taken deep within each flower's throat.

Yet you piece this world together
only to pick it apart, undoing nectar
from a stamen's base.
                              Your thin beak
pulls the thread of sweetness out—
you, who might be coaxed
to sip sugar-water from my tongue,
could I hold still long enough.

All too soon, my humming bird,
I *will* hold still long enough.

Promise me you'll
stitch my lips together.
Make of them

a blossom, closing.

All but Pedestrian

A leggy length of non-description, you're on the street
outside my house, walking north on Eleventh—
a man dressed in gray, in beige, in khaki,
the colors of this mid-January
slighted-of-light day.

Blending into Sellwood's concrete and still damp asphalt,
into its lichened bark, you're a mere flutter of motion
passing by. My eyes drift away from you.
Then veer back to rivet on what I see
as you head away.

With the heel you lift at each step's finish, you reveal
a red-bottomed shoe. Left to right to left: bursts
of carmine leather. Red heel and red shank.
Side to side, your underlining
flares into sight.

Wait just a minute, my eyes beg you, slow your gait.
Your feet have fledged *cardinals*, a matched pair.
Let me watch a little longer how they skim
the pavement, how they flit
along, in swoops—

as low as flying wild
will allow.

Today's November

—in this age of light pollution

Big leaf maple. Dogwood. Birch.
The leaves lift, fall,
flit and shudder away.

What crowded itself
to form summer's rampart of green
plucks itself bare, revealing a stark sky.

Come evening, I watch stripped trees
merge with that sky to make
one unbroken darkness.

No longer can I look up into night
and see bared limbs become
the dark veins feeding
a jeweled body of stars.

Each Seed

A smallest body sown
in the barrow. Bit of memory-bone.
The reliquary of color shape size.

A memento mori of mirror-life.
Archive for the ghosts of its every past.
Blueprint for each branching to follow.

From one seed a sum of life
spins backward. From that same seed
all flows forth. Easy enough

to think of the seed's green flame
carrying lives to come.
Not so easy to feel—

in the almost nothingness
of its self in my palm—
the weight of enough deaths

to overgrow this earth.

Nocturne

Asleep, I become a black river.
Flowers of darkness
cast their seed onto my banks,

while those earthly margins holding me
grow sotted from the touch
of my indigo tongue.

Take me into you, pinprick seed.
Let me swell your membranes,
soften your husks

until succulence breaks, blusters itself
toward bloom. An onrush,
I will soon become

the deep castoff
you loose into the air, that hypnosis
the world calls *perfume*.

Late Winter Rainbow

Unearthly visitor come close,
you are wide enough to light up
half the bleak day. You touch down
so near, I could fling open
the doors of this building and run
out into your seven bands
of glowing mist.

O half-hoop of luminous hues,
heaven has fallen
                  hard.

You are this sky's love letter—
spread open for all
our world to see.

Residence

Near their limb-brush
    their scruff and litter
    their warping bark
under their shade
    their aphid-drip
    their crow-hostel

close to the squirrel-sway
    resin liquor
    chartreuse light
not far from their wind-moan
    snow-sag
    sky-mottle
at the edge of their rain-routing:

I live in the green
    shrine of trees.

Interchange

The cedar breathes me in, exhales
a greener me. I pass through a crow's lungs,
the better for my journey.

Even the hummingbird—this one a plainer female—
trades with me a bit of the air making up
what we each, for a moment or two,
label as *self*.

The sky will soon take a breath
so big that nothing of me

will be given back.

Entreaty

Stones making this river's bed, I'm calling to you.
Stones rolling in water's rush, do you hear me?
The river carries its clamorous roil around and above you,
lighting up every hue and gleam of your skin.
Stones shifting under current's weight,
who among you is my own?

I've come to find out, to talk with the one of you
who is my kin. No, not true. Not entirely.
Ancestor-stone, you who have much to tell me,
I'm here to *listen* to what you say.

Give me the stories of our family fixations,
our immigrations—long journeys made on the back
of inching ice, wide diasporas accomplished
by the thaw of loose-limbed soil.

A child of gravel and riprap, daughter of your mineral tribe,
I'm headed back into the grit of my beginnings—
my bones ready to dissolve into rubble-dust.

Before I go, say it out loud. Tell me
my own stone name.

Where Is the Saint If Not in the Slightest of Things?

She could be the small brindle bug
creeping across my left sleeve-cuff.
The sight so startling
I jolt, flicking my wrist hard,
knowing I'll knock her off.
But don't, and so with my right hand
I cuff my cuff, flinging her to the oak floor.

She takes a few wobbling steps
and I speak to her—my apology. Of sorts.
Little Bug, why did I recoil at you
taking a walk on the Nepalese cotton
of my purple top? You are small,
and I am—in all truth—far less
than harmless.

With one soft fingertip, I brush her
onto a botanical postcard I've been using
as a bookmark. Now she rides
atop an image of a lemon plum branch
both in flower and in fruit.
For a few slow breaths, I keep level
these painted buds, blossoms,
and seed-swollen wombs, a platform
to carry her safely out the front door:
that fine balance the sacred requires.

I tip then tap the card, setting her
into the rain-damp garden,
beseeching this tiny saint to thrive—
green-fed in beatific mosses.

Blood Plum

On my bedside table the perfect
red plum would sit until it
wasn't. I was eight.
The plum, for then, ageless.
A vast plumbed roundness, it strained
against the air that was *not* it—once a white bloom
that went on to become a fruit gone beyond
the margin of being content with exactly
what it was.

I couldn't bring my teeth to break the sleek
of its skin. I foretold its spurt,
its smear, a shameless rivering
on my throat and chin.
I foresaw the stain, cerise—a blood
no fine-bristled scrub could remove.
I knew *whatever* I swallowed was then
no more.

I could barely bring my fingers to touch
the gleam of its cheek.
Unable to keep my hands to myself,
I traced the crease running a cleavage
down its swell. Surely that fruit
pulsed with some untold
heat. For certain, Eden was once
a whole orchard—limb-heavy plum trees
grown wild with bramble,
with thorns. I swore.
I would not take even
a taste.

A Furrier's Grandchild

Once I'd taken my first step,
my grandfather made me
a fur coat and matching hat.
White cony. My grandmother made
the lining. Pale satin to lie
between the pelt's napped underside
and my skin. In a year, I would
outgrow that cony coat.
But there would be others, each
just my ascended size. And hundreds
of customers' coats—the chinchilla,
mink, and Persian lamb I later tried on
in front of the fur shop's
triptych mirror. Their length
dragging the floor, their sleeves
overtaking my wrists and hands.

Each time I entered
an animal's skin, I could feel
the soft clutch of its death.
Cool. Sleek. Gleaming.
                    I stroked
            that terrible beauty.
Each time the animal let me peel it
away from my shoulders, let me
return its fallen weight to hang
from the rack's cold steel bar,
I emerged. Reborn.

An Unexpected Clearing

This air, cold. Trees, suddenly still.
The pine grove I'm walking through opens
into a clearing's cushiony duff.
At dead center: you lying
on your side, lifeless.

I catch and hold the cloud of my breath.
Looking down, my eyes slide
from your snout, to your ears,
to your guard hairs, umber and glinting.
No wound. No limb awry.
Fur unruffled. Nothing to disturb
your singular beauty.

No omnivore has found you.
Decay hasn't yet dared to make a move
on your sleek gleam—
you, some small, dark
nameless mammal.

I crouch myself closer,
only inches away. Craning my neck,
I now can see. There. In a single place
your fur flames out, making
a wildly gold gorget.

I do know who you are—Marten.
Only *your* stilled throat could still blaze
with the quick of what
you left behind
only cold minutes ago.

My Moon-Bridge

They say that ancestors visit us,
reaching where we live on earth
by walking down a rainbow's span.

But mine choose to walk a *moonbow*,
a white half-hoop made by lunar shine,
that arc connecting the moon
to my dreams while I sleep.

This moon-bridge is not without color,
but close. So be it. Long having frequented
thrift stores, yard sales, the nearest Goodwill,
I favor things dulled a shade by rub, paled by age.

Everyone knows: a dream is an old soul.
Dreams shine with what can be gained
only from *second-hand* light.

Proper Tribute

—Wind was the first person to inhabit the earth.
                                        —Navajo

East of the mountains, where I once lived,
wind blew most of the time.
Its strafe and chafe whittled me down.
In spring it blew the new-fangled green
right off the barely leafed trees.
In winter it sent braces of rain and snow
on horizontal journeys, seeing how long
it could keep them airborne
before letting them reach the ground.

I turned myself straight into its force
so my hair wouldn't whip my face.
I kept my head lowered.
Had I known then
who wind was,
I could have mustered
more attention, could have
paid my due respects.

I saw it shatter to pieces
a huge lake's surface. I saw how,
when it rose, the birds—
crows and grosbeaks, even the egrets—
disappeared. I could hear
the telephone lines singing
wind's day and night inside out
first-person meddlesome song.
Bowing my head even lower,
I could have at least
tried to hum along.

Written Kisses

The X's I sometimes make
below my signed name
are shorthand for the birds
artists at one time placed
around a love god's head.

Songbirds. Small. In flight.
Wings spread, bodies straight.
A chorus circling Eros. Singers
that people began to portray
as two bold pen-strokes.

A line from upper left
to bottom right, another
to cross it from high to low,
and I've set love
loose into the page's sky.

Thin black birds sing
the tunes learned as they flew
circles around the divine.
From under my name,
their inky voices rise.

Wearing the Sky

How can I count on
a clock's nonsense, its preening
split-second flicks,
when tonight's first star
will take at least
a million times my grasp of time
to find me with its light?

Whenever I stand under
a night-sky freighted
with those stars still alive or not,
my body's surface is lit
with billions of their gleam-points—
one for each burning cell
within me.

Inside and out, I am pied—
riddled with countless
dying fires.

Acknowledgments

With gratitude to the editors of the following publications in which these poems first appeared or are forthcoming, some in earlier versions:

Abandoned Mine: "Riches," "A Tree's Mirrored Self," "Where Is the Saint If Not in the Slightest of Things?"
Bangalore Review: "Yet Leafless, the Tulip Tree Readies To Flower"
Basalt: "Grave Goods"
The Birmingham Review: "A Furrier's Grandchild"
Bracken: "Wake"
Carolina Quarterly: "One of Yin's Voices Speaks Up" [as "Yin"]
Catamaran: "My Muse," "Wearing the Sky"
Cirque: "First Task"
Clackamas Literary Review: "Each Seed," "Lily"
Cloudbank: "Sown"
Come Shining, Essays and Poems on Writing in a Dark Time, edited by Jill Elliott and Alison Towle Moore, Kelson Books, 2017: "Reparations"
A Constellation of Kisses, edited by Diane Lockward, Terrapin Books, 2019: "Written Kisses"
The Evergreen Review: "Omen," "Urine," "A Wife's Belated Bow To the Sun"
Fireweed: "Pursued by What Frightens Her," "You, Coreopsis"
Hubbub: "A Backstory Beyond My Recounting"
The Inflectionist Review: "Household," "To My Coffin-Tree"
Mudlark: "Entreaty," "Interchange," "Late Winter Rainbow," "Nocturne," "Residence"
The Poeming Pigeon: A Journal of Poetry & Art (forthcoming in Issue 13): "Today's November"
Poetry Online: "Ophelia Speaks of the Stream That Inhabits Her Dreams"
The RavensPerch: "If I Were Money," "If My People Had Totems, My Pole Would Include," "Inhabited," "Unfurling," "The World After"
Tikkun: "Kinship"
Weber, the Contemporary West: "The Gardener Learns To Live under Water," [as "How I Learn to Live under Water"], "Proper Tribute"
Windfall: "All But Pedestrian"

A version of "Downfall" is one part of the libretto of Eriks Esenvalds' three-movement choral composition "Naming the Rain."

"Wearing the Sky" was the spoken text in Jayanthi Raman's Sanchari Abhinaya solo performance as part of her 2022 *Margam: the Divine Path* dance concert.

With gratitude to Fran Adler, Maggie Chula, Christine Delea, Gerry Foote, Cindy Gutiérrez, Diane Holland, Andrea Hollander, Mike Langtry, Judy Montgomery, John Morrison, Donna Prinzmetal, Willa Schneberg, Penelope Schott, and Dianne Stepp for their comments on some of these poems.

PAULANN PETERSEN, Oregon Poet Laureate Emerita, has seven previous full-length books of poetry. Her poems have appeared in many journals and anthologies, including *Poetry, Prairie Schooner, The Birmingham Review, Catamaran, Tikkun*, the Internet's *Poetry Daily*, and *POETRY IN MOTION*, which placed poems on the Tri-met busses and lightrail cars in the Portland area. The Latvian composer Eriks Esenvalds has chosen her poems as the lyrics for four of his choral compositions, including the song that ends the award-winning Latvian film Es Esmu Šeit and— most recently—his three-part song cycle *Naming the Rain*. She was a Stegner Fellow at Stanford University. In 2006 she received the Holbrook Award from Oregon Literary Arts, and in 2013, Willamette Writers' Distinguished Northwest Writer Award. As Oregon's 6th Poet Laureate, she traveled over 27,500 miles within Oregon, visiting all of its 36 counties to give workshops, readings, and presentations at schools, libraries, and community centers.

Photo: Sam Blair

salmonpoetry

Cliffs of Moher, County Clare, Ireland

"Publishing the finest Irish and international literature."
Michael D. Higgins, President of Ireland